SUFFOLK COAST
FROM THE AIR 3
THE EVER-CHANGING SHORE

Mike Page

HALSGROVE

Title page: The view above Corton.

First published in Great Britain in 2015

Copyright © 2015 Mike Page

British Library Cataloguing-in-Publication Data
A CIP record for this title is available from the British Library

ISBN 978 0 85704 278 1

HALSGROVE
Halsgrove House,
Ryelands Business Park,
Bagley Road, Wellington, Somerset TA21 9PZ
Tel: 01823 653777   Fax: 01823 216796
email: sales@halsgrove.com

Part of the Halsgrove group of companies
Information on all Halsgrove titles is available at: www.halsgrove.com

Printed in China by Everbest Printing Co Ltd

FOREWORD

When I first met Mike Page prior to publishing his first book, *A Broads-Eye View*, well over a decade ago, he was very much a pioneer in developing techniques to take professional-quality aerial photographs from a light aircraft. His determination to achieve the best possible images, using relatively modest equipment, made it feasible to publish his first book, and the others that followed, at prices people could afford. Since that first meeting it has been a privilege to work closely with him and to play some small part in establishing Mike's name as the go-to man whenever aerial photographs of the region are called for.

Mike is indeed 'Mr Aerial Photography' of East Anglia, producing films, books, newspaper and magazine features, along with providing assistance to local authorities and individuals in need of up-to-date aerial images. Those who know Mike well will also know that his enthusiasm and determination to come up with the best photographs is coupled with a modesty and generosity that sees all of his remunerative work going to help charitable causes.

The best contemporary aerial photographers, those who produce images for public view, look beyond the pure technical quality of their pictures. They search too for an aesthetic content that provides that vital element of pleasurable surprise: the slanting shadows that add a three-dimensional quality to the landscape, towering cloudscapes on far horizons, reflected sunlight from mirror-like Broads or waves breaking upon the shore. Mike has an artist's eye. His close-up of the 'whale' on page 52 and the mudflats on page 99, transformed into the delicate tendrils of an alien plant, bring to us a whole new awareness of our fragile world.

And of course, on our eastern seaboard, we are increasingly reminded of the threat posed by the encroaching sea. Few have done more than Mike to bring the actuality of these startling changes sharply into focus and, for this alone, he deserves our appreciation. His pictures reveal to us things that are normally hidden from view and surprise us when we find that what we had imagined the layout of the land to be is in reality quite different. And along with the changes that have taken place, we are also reminded of things that have remained unchanged.

Within the next few years it is quite possible that anyone who wishes to do so will be able, for a modest sum, to purchase a drone pilotless aircraft and use it to take aerial pictures of reasonable quality. And no doubt such pictures will increasingly become available on the internet and social media sites. Consequently there will be important questions for the authorities to answer regarding security, invasion of privacy and, not least, the safety concerns relating to commercial aircraft and other pilots currently controlled by stringent and long-standing air-safety laws.

But whatever the future may hold, Mike's legacy will endure not least through his books and the thousands of superb aerial photographs now in his archive; images that will continue to amaze, delight and inform future generations.

Simon Butler
The Publisher
Halsgrove 2015

Mistley and Manningtree are in Essex. The county boundary between Suffolk and Essex runs alongside the quay on this picture.

Looking west along the Stour from New Mill Creek, Stutton.

Left:
From Cattawade, the county boundary follows the course of the River Stour all the way to Haverhill.

The Royal Hospital School at Holbrook
with Alton Water in the background.

Holbrook village looking north.

Harkstead village looking north-east.

Erwarton Creek and Erwarton Bay still retain a very small area of saltmarsh.

Right:
A great view along the Stour looking west with Parkeston Quay, Harwich, on the left (south) bank and Shotley Gate on the right (north) bank.

The derelict site of HMS *Ganges*. This is all that remains of the Naval Training School for boys wanting to join the Royal Navy. This shore base closed in 1976. Interestingly the author's father, Royal Arthur John Watson Page started training for the Royal Navy at HMS *Ganges*, joining the establishment at the age of 18 in November 1918, but there lies another story.

Left:

Shotley Gate and Shotley Point Marina

Right:

Beautifully positioned at Shotley Point, the Shotley Marina provides 350 fully-serviced berths and has a lock that allows craft to enter or leave on all states of the tide.

Left:

Looking north-west along the River Orwell with Collimer Point centre of picture and Felixstowe Port on the bottom right.

Right:

The Thames barge *Reminder* a familiar sight around the Suffolk and Essex coast. *Reminder* was built at Mistley and launched in 1929.

Levington Marina (Suffolk Yacht Harbour) on the north bank of the River Orwell has a capacity of 550 craft on fully-serviced berths.

Woolverstone Hall is a magnificent Grade I listed building set in 84 acres of lush Suffolk parkland on the south bank of the River Orwell.

Left:

Pin Mill on the south bank of the River Orwell, with the Orwell Bridge and Ipswich in the background.

Ipswich Docks are thriving, handling around two million tonnes of freight each year. Operated by Associated British Ports, eight ships are loading or unloading at the time this picture was taken.

Ipswich looking north over the A14 and the Orwell Bridge.

Ipswich Haven Marina which is accessed through a lock. The River Orwell veers off left of picture.

Toward the sea from the Orwell Bridge.

Svendborg Maersk leaves the quayside at Felixstowe bound for the sea.

Part of the recently constructed berths 8 and 9 at Port of Felixstowe. Further extension to this area is currently in progress which will increase the combined length of berths 8 and 9 to 920 metres and include three new cranes.

Sunset over Felixstowe.

A view over the port with Shotley Gate and the River Stour beyond.

Left: Landguard Point looking west.

Landguard Point looking north-east.

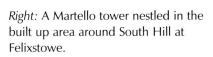

Right: A Martello tower nestled in the built up area around South Hill at Felixstowe.

Felixstowe prides itself on its golden beaches and the attractions in the area around the pier.

Cobbolds Point protected from erosion by rock and fishtail groynes.

Felixstowe Ferry Golf Club, established in 1880, enjoys fabulous views over the Deben estuary.

The ever-changing sandbanks at the mouth of the River Deben.

Felixstowe Ferry. Some buildings (as early as 1043) have been recorded on the site of this small fishing village.

Remaining saltmarsh on the River Deben.

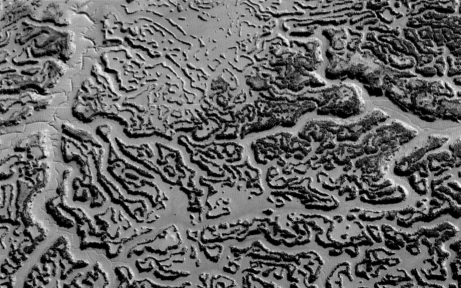

Ramsholt Quay. An ideal spot by the river adjacent to the Ramsholt Arms.

Right:
Waldringfield is mentioned in the Domesday Book. It lies within the Suffolk Coasts and Heaths, a designated Area of Outstanding Natural Beauty.

Woodbridge Tide Mill, built in 1793, last worked commercially in 1957. It is open to the public.

Left:
Looking north-north-west toward Woodbridge.

Martlesham Creek (bottom of picture) with Woodbridge in the distance.

Looking down the River Deben from overhead Bromeswell. The bridge in the foreground carries the A1152.

From 2000 feet there's a spectacular view of the Deben showing both Felixstowe Ferry and Bawdsey Manor.

Left: One of my favourite views of the Deben as it meanders down to the sea.

The 1953 floods devastated great swathes of the east coast of England. Compare this with the picture below, taken in 2015.

Three rivers, Stour, Orwell and Deben from high above Bawdsey looking south-west.

Bawdsey Manor, built in the late 1890s, was acquired by the Air Ministry in 1936 and used for the further development of radar.

St Mary's church with its Norman tower was the dedicated church of RAF Bawdsey. It is a mere 920 metres from the sea. The proceeds from the sale of land to build the houses of Cavell Close (foreground) funded the new sea defences.

Left: Bawdsey was used as an RAF missile site and was active throughout the cold war period until the 1990s. Bloodhound missiles occupied the concrete pads. The station closed in March 1991.

Left:

Wartime clifftop relics now swallowed by the sea.

East Lane, Bawdsey, with a view of Hollesley Bay curving into Orford Ness.
Sizewell B's white dome is in the distance.

Right:

The Bawdsey 'Bonio'; the terminal groyne named
after a dog biscuit, protects Martello Y and the soft
cliffs from erosive scour.

Shingle Street and Weir Point guarding the entrance to the River Ore.

Shingle Street. An incredible shingle area, beautifully shaped by the sea and ever changing.

In December 2013 the tidal surge brought much flooding and coastal damage to Suffolk. This view shows Shingle Street almost as an island.

Left: The mouth of the River Ore. Weir Point is top right of picture. Ever-changing sandbanks and tides can be a real challenge for sailors.

The River Ore and Orfordness.

The Butley River looking from Butley Mill toward the River Ore, the sea lying beyond.

Two of the three Martello towers along the west bank of the River Ore with different conversions. The third (below left) is still virtually original.

Fishing near the fast-running tides and changing sandbanks of North Weir Point.

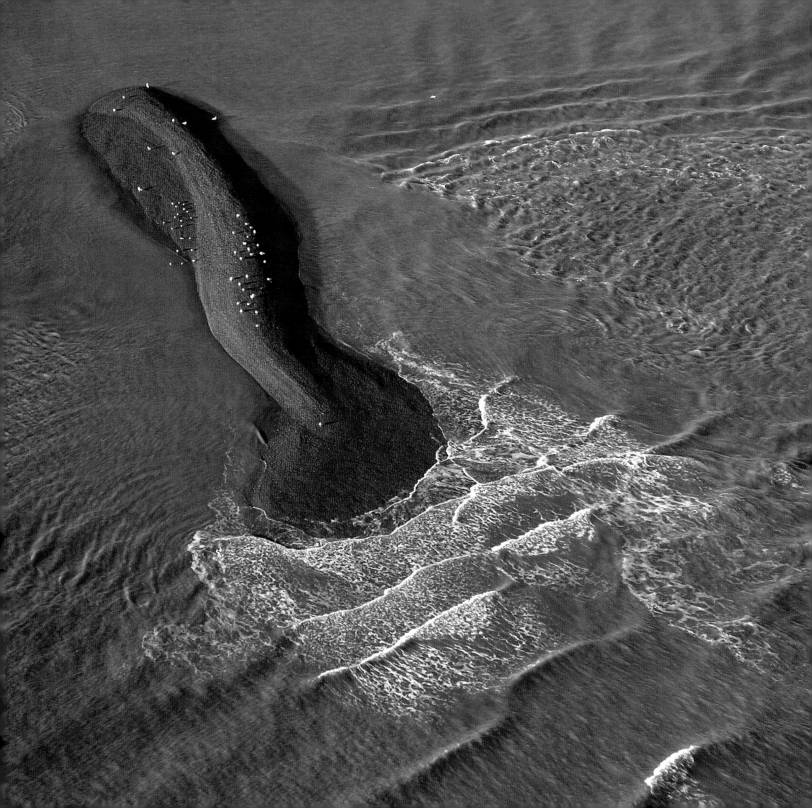

Left:

Sandbank in the Ore mouth resembling a whale.

Right:

Havergate Island RSPB after the 7 December 2013 tidal surge.

Below:

Havergate Island RSPB as it usually looks.

All that remains of Orford Castle is the polygonal keep which has walls ten feet thick. The finest Norman keep in Great Britain.

Left:
Orford from Stonyditch Point.

Saint Bartholomew, Orford.

Right:
Orford Quay.

Orford looking north-west toward Tunstall Forest.

Looking north-east from Orford toward Aldeburgh.

Orford Ness.

Left: One of the watch towers close to the lighthouse at Orfordness. Erosion caused it to topple in May 2014.

The Orfordness lighthouse, December 2004.

The same scene but in February 2015. Note the erosion and the owner's attempt at sea defence. When will the lighthouse lean like the watchtower?

The storm surge of December 2013 flooded large areas of Lantern Marshes to the north of the lighthouse.

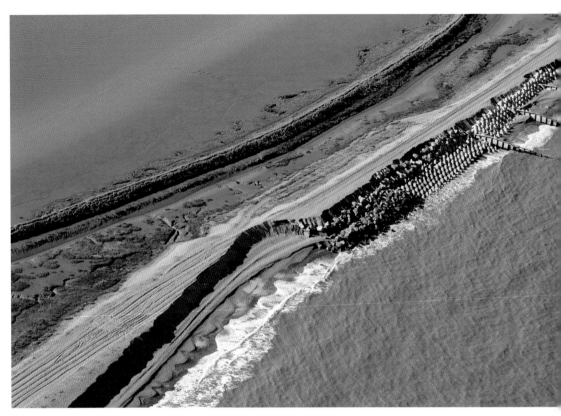

The shingle bank almost breached during the December 2013 tidal surge.

Left:
Sudbourne Beach, part of the narrow shingle bank that separates the sea from the River Alde.

The River Alde looking west from Slaughden.

Iken with Snape Maltings in the distance.

St Botolph's church, Iken.

Right:
The River Alde leading down to Aldeburgh, with Snape Maltings foreground.

Barbers Point, Hazlewood Marshes, was breached by the December 2013 surge putting nearby properties at risk.

Surge damage to the river wall. The picture shows water running off the flooded area at low tide.

Aldeburgh.

Looking north from Aldeburgh toward Thorpeness.

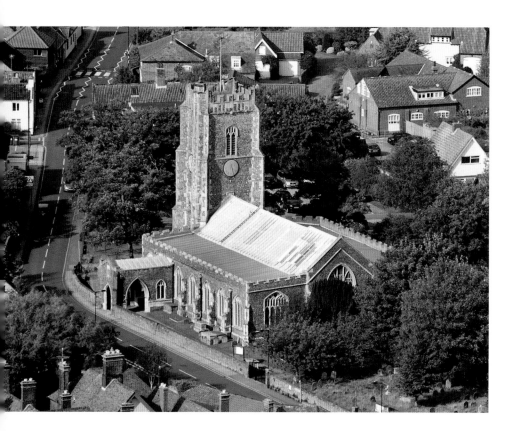

The church of St Peter and St Paul, Aldeburgh.

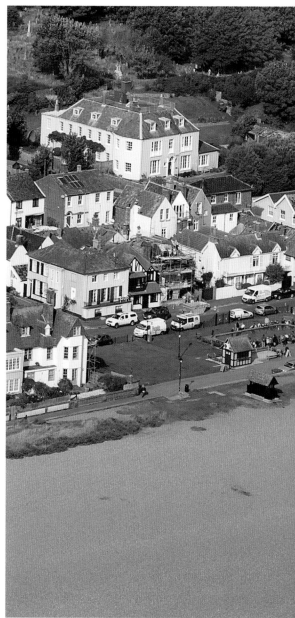

Right:
Aldeburgh's Moot Hall (seen centre) was in the heart of town before erosion took away many buildings. It has been used as a prison and also a town hall in previous centuries.

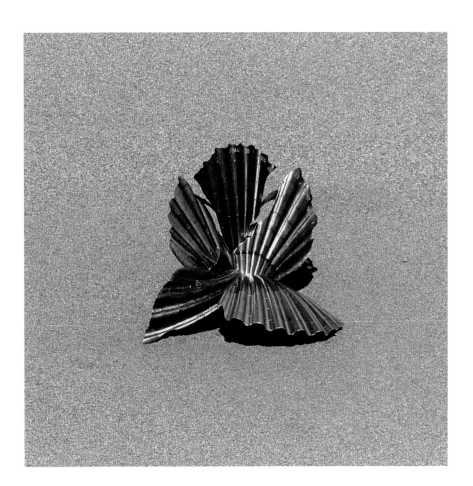

The 13 foot high Scallop Shell sculpture by Maggi Hambling, installed in 2003, lies on the shore just north of Aldeburgh. It is a memorial to Benjamin Britten, the Lowestoft-born composer.

Left:
Aldeburgh looking south over the Alde, Ore and beautiful Suffolk.

Aldeburgh North Warren nature reserve, RSPB.

Thorpeness showing the Ness north of the village.

The Tudor-style gatehouse at picturesque Thorpeness, once a water tower.

Left:

Thorpeness Mere, where rowing boats and canoes can be hired for a trip on the lake.

Sizewell power station looking south.

Sizewell A, left of picture, has been decommissioned. The domed Sizewell B is to the right.

The grassed area north of the dome is the future site for Sizewell C. Minsmere RSPB reserve and Dunwich Forest are seen centre picture.

Minsmere, the jewel of the RSPB reserves, and host to the BBC television series Springwatch in early 2015.

Minsmere RSPB reserve looking west.

Coastguard Cottages (National Trust) on Dunwich Heath cliffs. Thousands of visitors come here each year to enjoy a snack in the tearooms.

Right:
Cliff House Holiday Park at Dunwich with wonderful views of the sea.

Left: Dunwich looking north with Dingle Marshes beyond the village.

Part of Greyfriars, a ruined Franciscan friary and leper hospital lies on the clifftop at Dunwich.

Right: St James' church, Dunwich.

The Flora Tearooms, Dunwich, a notable venue for fish and chips on the East Suffolk coast.

Right:
Looking south over Dunwich toward Minsmere and Sizewell.

Left: The flooding of Dingle Marshes in December 2013 after the tidal surge.

Westwood Marshes in winter.

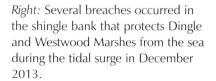

Right: Several breaches occurred in the shingle bank that protects Dingle and Westwood Marshes from the sea during the tidal surge in December 2013.

The River Blyth with Walberswick left.

Walberswick looking north-east with Southwold in the distance.

St Andrew's church, Walberswick, is the fourth church to be built on this site with the current
building standing inside the ruins of the third.

Right:
Southwold Harbour, Walberswick on the left.

Left: Looking south from above Walberswick with Dunwich Forest centre picture and the wide sweep of Sole Bay to the left.

Snow shrouds the landscape around the River Blyth and Walberswick.

Right: Low tide on the Blyth mudflats.

Holy Trinity church, Blythburgh, known as The Cathedral of the Marshes.

Left: The River Blyth at Blythburgh looking east.

Another gem along the Suffolk Coast, Southwold.

Reydon looking south-east toward Southwold.

A friend of the author's in his autogyro has taken centre stage passing Southwold on this photo sortie along the coast.

Right:
Southwold Pier.

Looking south over Southwold.

Properties on Easton Lane at Easton Bavents, February 2005.

Ten years later and this photograph, taken in February 2015, shows the amount of cliff lost to erosion.

Easton Broad and marshland, designated a Special Area of Conservation, is gradually disappearing under the sea.

Right: Death by salt air and saltwater.

Covehithe Broad also is eroding. It's designated a Special Area of Conservation along with Easton Broad and Benacre Broad.

Covehithe enveloped by early morning sea fog.

St Andrew's church, Covehithe.

Right:
A view north along the coast from Benacre Broad with Kessingland Ness and Lowestoft in the distance.

Benacre Broad, a favorite birdwatching spot for many people.

Left: The sea continually erodes the cliffs at Benacre and occasionally reveals the unexpected. These are Second World War underground buildings; their original purpose is unknown.

The ploughed field provides a startling pictorial measure of the rate of erosion along this part of the Suffolk Coast. Here in 1994...

...and twenty years on. This picture was taken in 2014.

Kessingland wind turbines visible from Beach Farm Benacre.

Right: The Hundred River weaves it way toward Henstead from Benacre Sluice pumping station. Without more defences the sea will break through at this point on the coast and will flood thousands of acres of arable farmland.

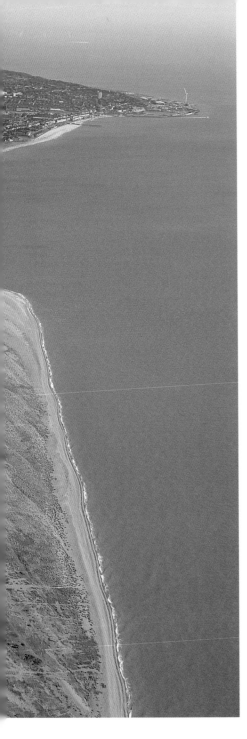

Kessingland's two wind turbines, the subject of much controversy.

Left: Kessingland with Lowestoft beyond.

A very popular car boot sale is held in the shadow of the Kessingland turbines.

The former Pakefield Lighthouse, now the home of Coastwatch.

Pakefield, with small fishing boats drawn up along the beach.

The two churches of All Saints and St Margaret's, virtually on the beach at Pakefield, shared a site but onced served two parish communities worshipping separately.

Pakefield looking south.

Lowestoft from overhead Pakefield, with snow showers over the sea.

Claremont Pier and Lowestoft Harbour.

The harbour and lake at Lothing

The bridge is a subject of much controversy and causes huge traffic problems. An extra river crossing is proposed.

Left: The headquarters of Lowestoft Cruising Club on Lake Lothing. Traces of snow on the ground and boats hauled out showing that it 's winter.

Left: The extent of Lake Lothing is clearly visible from 4000ft. Note also the route of the old railway track from Lowestoft to Great Yarmouth showing clearly.

Wind turbine nicknamed Gulliver.

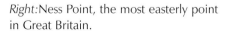

Right: Ness Point, the most easterly point in Great Britain.

Oulton Broad in the late 1950s

Left:
Oulton Broad with (foreground) Lake Lothing.

Mutford Lock enables boats to pass between Oulton Broad (left) & Lake Lothing.

Lowestoft High Light (installed 1874); there has been a light here since the 1660s.

Gunton cliffs north
of Lowestoft.

A caravan park lies close to the edge of the cliffs at Corton, but what superb views they must have.

RAF Hopton was opened in July 1940 as part of the Chain Home radar system similar to that at Bawdsey. The site remained operational until 1997 and was finally put up for sale in 2000 when it was sold to a private purchaser.

Looking south toward Lowestoft from the county boundary with Norfolk, marked with a red line bottom right.

Hopton adjoins the county boundary but is in Norfolk.

I had to include Hopton as a massive sea defence scheme has just been completed. This defence work may signal some similar work further south at Corton as it seems successful at recovering the beaches.

Below: Constructing the fishtail groynes at Hopton.

The completed defence scheme of nine fishtail groynes and cliff base repairs at Hopton, looking toward Great Yarmouth.